RECYCLED PARSNIPS

Rhymes and doodles for

non-grown-ups

Mikey O'Crikey

www.mikeyocrikey.com

Rhymes and doodles are copyright of Mikey O'Crikey. So no passing any of it off as your own. Especially you, Bernard. I know your tricks… Anyway, here's the rest of the boring bit…

ISBN-13: 9798560560270

"A little nonsense now and then
is relished by the wisest men."

- WILLY WONKA

Contents

TIP 1... If you see one of these , it means the rhyme continues over the page...

TIP 2... Try reading the rhymes outloud to your family, friends, teacher, postman, lollipop lady...

Foreword

This book's made of recycled parsnips,

Go on, have a sniff.

It has that slightly sweet aroma,

And an ever-so earthy whiff.

I could have made it from turnips,

But they give the page a tint,

Of reddish brown, so to read the words,

You really have to squint.

So, I made it out of parsnips,

The best veg for printing text.

You can pull it back from your nose now,

Turn the page, find out what's next...

ECTAPONG

Oh what it is to set upon,

A jolly game of ectapong.

That most bright of racquet sports,

Played by tall, behatted sorts.

The first to serve - the one who calls,

What's heavier, the bat or balls?

You see, they either play with rocks,

Or several pairs of rolled up socks.

Held upon a flat-ish ledge,

Adorned with twigs and bits of hedge.

To gain a point, the ball must roll,

Right past the shrew but hit the vole...

...and bounce into your rival's pocket,

Unless they can return or block it.

And so one player wins the crown,

When the other's trousers fall right down.

So what it is to set upon,

A jolly game of ectapong.

That most bright of racquet sports,

Just wear your cleanest boxer shorts.

The Fastest Gumstringer in the West

She was the Fastest Gumstringer in the West,

That's what they say, the very best.

An ace, a master, the champ, the boss,

With a line of ordinary dental floss.

She could clean her whole mouth in a sprint,

Though could often only taste spearmint.

You see all that practice does no favours,

For experiencing a variety of flavours.

But she could dig out all sorts of grit,

From porridge oats to bacon bits.

Things that are just beyond belief,

Would emerge from between those teeth.

I once witnessed to my revulsion,

When with quite impressive propulsion,

From her gob the floss flicked out,

A fully intact Brussel sprout.

5

RECYCLED
FISH SUPPER

I hear she fished with her stringy rod,

A whole portion of battered cod.

Complete with mushy peas of course,

And, fittingly, some tartare sauce.

Now with these skills to shift detritus,

She ensured no sign of gingivitis.

And she never needed a single filling,

So no dentist from her would earn a shilling.

6

That said she would make chemists cheer,

For she'd use up miles of floss each year.

It caused her piggy bank infliction,

As she couldn't get it on prescription.

But then the only kind of plaque she knew,

Was on her childhood home and coloured blue.

See she was well-renowned for being blessed,

As the Fastest Gumstringer in the West.

Mister Mooch

Poor Mister Mooch, the disgruntled old pooch,

Fed up with bones and loud telephones.

Tired of his house and the resident mouse,

That scratches and sneaks and frequently squeaks.

He can't stand the kitties who tease him with ditties,

The mocking meows, he answers with growls.

They jump and they dance, around him they prance,

With nose in the air, stray near if they dare.

The same boring grub everyday in a tub,

That hasn't been washed since Napoleon was boshed.

The pats and the strokes from the local old folks,

Who spit past their gums cold tea and cake crumbs.

But far worst of all is the vet Dr Scrawl,

Who's covered in nits and smells of armpits.

He pokes and he prods and he tuts and he nods,

Poor Mister Mooch, the disgruntled old pooch.

Beans on Toast

Oh, beans on toast, beans on toast,

So much better than a Sunday roast.

Lots more flavour than a bag of chips,

And will fill you fuller than some crisps with dips.

Oh, toast with beans, toast with beans,

No challenge madam from your salad greens.

Broccoli is yummier? You're joking mate!

There's no contest for what I'm putting on my plate.

Oh, the toast is buttered and the beans are baked,

Better for our tummies when we're first awaked.

Has the whole day to moosh inside our bellies,

Build up the gases for some nighttime smellies.

Oh, beans on toast, beans on toast,

The meal it's safe to say that I love the most.

No question, hands down, for me it's the winner,

So give me beans on toast for breakfast, lunch and dinner.

ALLERCHEESE

Hay fever, I have a spot of that,
Get itchy when I'm near a cat.
But whatever happens, please, please, please,
Don't let me get no allercheese.

If nothing made my nose go redder,
Than a lovely lump of mature cheddar,
I think I'd be so sad I'd cry,
Into my dairy-free cheese pie.

And no itching would make me moan louder,

Than a rash I'd got from grated gouda.

Or if I had to pay a digestive price,

For having a halloumi slice.

There really are few joys quite sweeter,

Than mozzarella on a margherita.

With no cheese a pizza it would not be,

In particular the quattro formaggi.

A Greek salad would not be better,

If it was missing crumbly clumps of feta.

Or cheesecake with no mascarpone,

And what would you do with macaroni?

For fewer things I more loudly cheer,

Than big cubes of tandooried paneer.

And not many snacks will lift my day,

Like toast topped with tons of fromage frais.

Thus if from my diet I had to ban,

Port salut or parmesan,

Or any other cheese I like,

I think I'd go on hunger strike.

For without it what would lunch be built on?

No emmental, no brie or stilton...

So listen up body, don't you dare,

Make me sneeze on the camembert.

What the Cow Thought About the Rain

She looked up to the clouds so high,

Blinking as they hit her eye,

Plopping one then two then three,

Raindrops scooped up from the sea.

She did not know this part of course,

For she was bovine, not a horse.

Gee-gees are the clever ones,

They're especially talented with puns.

16

"Hey," said one horse to his mate.

"Ed, I'm eating - can't it wait?"

"No, *the hay* - it's getting wet."

"It'll be that rain again, I bet."

But all the cow could say was "Moo".

(Cows can't talk, I thought you knew).

Who knows if she likes wet or dry,

Oh well, soon she'll be a pie.

Blasteroids

Two players, two racquets, one ball,

On a court not especially small.

The game starts with a thwack,

And you lob forth and back,

Yet an out there is never to call.

No umpire, no ball girls or boys,

And played neither by dukes nor viceroys.

No one eats a banana,

Nor wears a bandana,

And you serve with no particular poise.

You are never at risk of a let,

As, you see, there's no sign of a net.

One could try an ace,

Risk a ball to the face,

But it quite likely will lead to regret.

It's not entirely like tennis you see,

The rules only are as you agree.

It's called blasteroids,

Just best one avoids,

To run backwards and headbutt a tree.

Olympicking

I'm trying out for the Olympics,

But not yet sure which sport.

Will it be the track or field,

The pool or pitch or court?

So many things to choose from,

It's really hard to pick,

Whether to run around in circles,

Or throw a very pointy stick.

Dive off a board in tandem?

For that I'd need a chum.

Don't like the look of hop, skip, jump,

You land right on your bum.

I could try to be a gymnast,

A triathlete or cycler.

But that all seems rather tiring,

And I don't look good in Lycra.

For some you need to ride a horse,

But I can't be fussed with that.

And I'm sure it must be frowned on,

To do dressage on a cat.

How about windsurfing?

Could be the ocean sports for me.

But then it's tricky to get in practice,

When living nowhere near the sea.

A river event instead perhaps?
Canoeing. That's it, I'm sold!
Though I have a knack for capsizing,
Which makes it tough to win the gold.

Got it! This idea's perfect,
Knew I'd get it sooner or later.
I'll sit back, put my feet up,
And be a champion spectator.

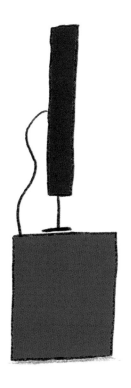

Silent but Deadly

I caught a spider that was hiding,
In the bathroom, by the loo.
The little blighter was just sat there,
As I had my morning poo.

I trapped him under a toilet roll,
Thinking he could be my chum.
But when I lifted up the roll a bit,
He turned and showed his bum.

Then, though I didn't hear a thing,

I could soon detect a trace,

Of digested flies, I'm certain,

He'd just farted in my face!

I tell you, his bite could not be worse,

Than that smell, that stench, that stink.

So I put him back and left him,

By the loo, beneath the sink.

Billy Bread-and-Butter-Pants

Billy Bread-and-Butter Pants,

He ate so much dessert,

That he couldn't fit into his shorts,

His sweater or his shirt.

He couldn't tie his tie on,

Because his neck had got so wide.

His belt didn't fit his belly,

For all the pudding there inside.

He couldn't slip his socks on,

The pud had even reached his toes.

Which meant he'd struggle to put on

His shoes either I suppose.

He went to have a shower,

But the curtain wouldn't surround him.

So he had to use the garden hose,

Which is really quite astounding.

He tried on his dad's trousers,

But even those were a torment.

So he went into the garden shed,

To dig out the family tent.

Out the bag he took that canvas,

And he threw it round his frame.

But then a pole upped and lodged itself,

In place I shall not name.

His parents' bed sheets were his last resort,

So he dressed in those for school.

And when he turned up to his class,

He didn't half look quite the fool.

Soon he was his usual size again,

But he had learnt from his mistake.

You really rather rarely need,

That second slice of cake.

Snot, Sweat and Cheese

I myself would rather not

Swim in a pool that's full of snot.

Think of all the bogies in there,

They'd float into your trunks and get stuck in your hair.

Also, I beg you must never let

Me fall into a vat of armpit sweat.

Especially if it's that of Mr Meacher,

He must be the planet's smelliest teacher.

But most of all, please, please, please

Keep me away from toenail cheese.

With crackers for lunch would be the worst,

I'd go so green, I think I'd burst!

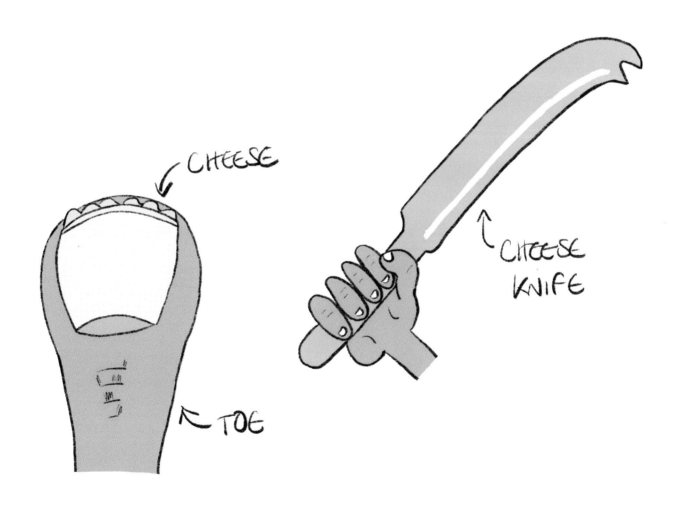

CHEESE

TOE

CHEESE
KNIFE

The Confectionery Kid

I heard about an outlaw,
Who had a Bounty on his head.
He had two Twixes in his boots,
And Maltesers in his bed.

He had Smarties in his underpants,
Honestly, he did.
For he was known across the West,
As the Confectionery Kid.

32

He went to rob a stagecoach,

Heard there was a fortune he could steal.

But when he got there all he found,

Was a half-eaten Wagon Wheel.

A posse came a-chasing him,

All the way from old Tombstone.

They'd been persuaded by the sheriff,

With big bars of Toblerone.

They caught up with him in Texas,
He had fled across three states.
But hadn't secured his saddle bag,
And left a trail of After Eights.

They found him in a saloon bar,
Things didn't half get punchy.
Until he distracted the whole posse,
With a Snickers and a Crunchie.

Then on his old horse, Toffee Crisp,

He fled down to Mexico.

Where he began a pinata making school,

And picked a liquorice banjo.

They sent Texas Rangers down to find him,

But not a single one of them did.

No one heard another Wispa,

Of the Confectionery Kid.

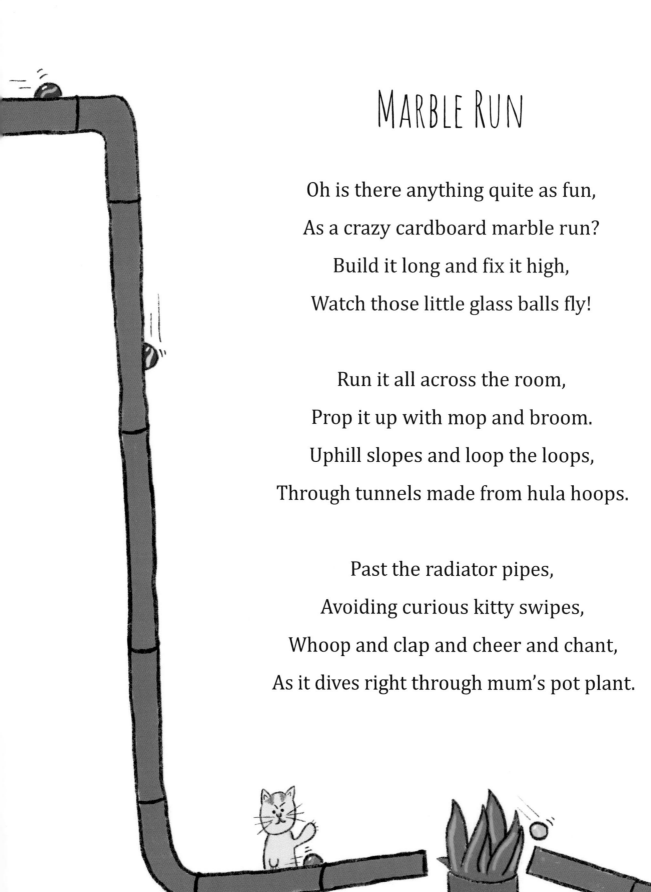

Marble Run

Oh is there anything quite as fun,
As a crazy cardboard marble run?
Build it long and fix it high,
Watch those little glass balls fly!

Run it all across the room,
Prop it up with mop and broom.
Uphill slopes and loop the loops,
Through tunnels made from hula hoops.

Past the radiator pipes,
Avoiding curious kitty swipes,
Whoop and clap and cheer and chant,
As it dives right through mum's pot plant.

Roll two down, or three or four,

Shucks, why not roll down even more?

And if you find you overdo it,

Just get out the craft box and re-glue it.

Folks lose their marbles, so I hear,

The bloke next door lost his last year.

They must have dropped from run to floor,

And rolled right out his kitchen door.

But if mine were lost I'd just use peas,

Or conkers from horse chestnut trees.

Because there's no way I'm missing all the fun,

Of a crazy cardboard marble run!

Scrobble

From a bag fish 7 tiles,

Plonk them in a row.

A mix of consonants and vowels,

Go on, let's have a go.

BUMTZYL, for 23.

Now a definition please...

It's the posterior warmth you get when sat

In a pool of melted cheese.

For a score of just 14,

My word is UPITELEK.

A cross of rhino and giraffe,

It has a very bendy neck.

CHEEEQE and on a double word,

That's a score of 42.

It's the noise of a halloumi sandwich

Being eaten by a shrew.

CONKSQTL for 24,

The small grunt you make mid-squat.

No, I think you'll find it is in fact

A metric measurement for snot.

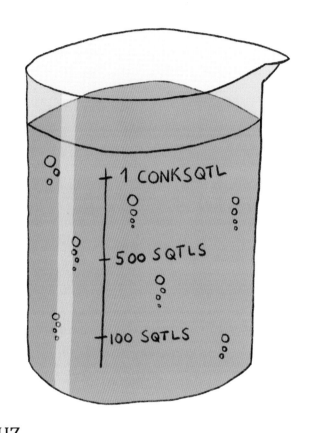

21 for ROMPISUZ,

What nuns nickname their knickers.

Around convents you'll hear it whispered,

But it's not often said by vicars.

KOBIQUOZ (a cosmic term),

And times two for 64!

Where'd you get the extra Q and Z?

We've used both twice before...

FLUMMIUX I say to you!

Who cares about the rules?

By the way, that's a slang term

For the Queen of Sheba's jewels.

UMPLIOID for a mere 13,

They say bad luck for some.

Uh huh, too right, you said it pal,

It's a boil on a builder's bum!

For a 20 pointer, YUPIFUTS,

A double letter on the Y.

When you, by mistake, add fish fingers

To your ham and cabbage pie.

OOMBLPIT, a not oft spoke word,

Just 12 points but it's a doozy.

It's the little well that traps dead skin

At the bottom of a jacuzzi.

Your final go, I'm in the lead,

So you better make it wowzers.

UBAYIKES - when your granddad

Drops a cactus down his trousers.

Animal Tragic

Said Pete to Fred "What's wrong with your head?!
You've lost one ear and your nose!"
"A woodpecker's to blame," Fred mumbled in shame,
"I must look like a tree I suppose."

Said Fred to Pete "And look at your feet!
Where on Earth have all your toes gone?!"
"I was attacked by a slug," said Pete with a shrug,
"While sunbathing on the lawn."

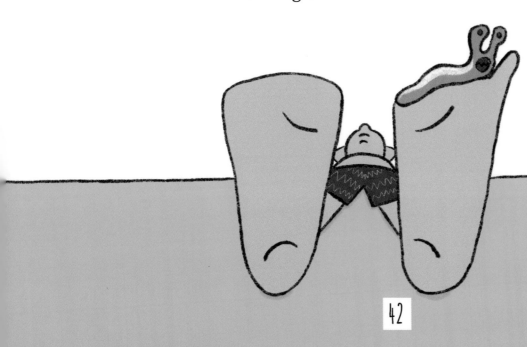

"That's nothing," said Pat, overhearing their chat,
"My buttocks were nicked by four shrews.
Now to sit comfortably they've strapped cushions to me,
Which is awkward when I want number twos."

The Man Who Had Three Armpits

Oh a smelly smelly man was he,
He had three armpits, do you see?
See, he'd not the same as me and you,
You've just the two pits, as I do.

Do you know where his third was?
Wasn't where you'd think because,
Because you'd think it near a limb,
Limbs, well, he'd just four on him.

LIMB 1   LIMB 2   LIMB 3   LIMB 4

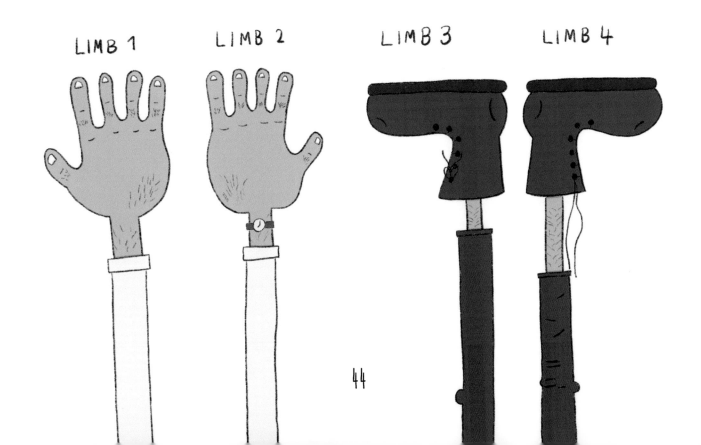

Him's extra pit, or *his* I should say,

Say, it just up and appeared one day.

Day turned to night, it was still there,

There on his face that else was fair.

Fair he'd been and a cleanly sir,

Sir who once a son he were.

Were indeed, he had a mum,

Mum taught him to wash face and bum.

Bum's are simple enough to clean,

Cleaning his face now, well I mean…

Mean folk of course would oft point out,

Out his face long hairs would sprout.

Sprouting hairs don't make a beard,

Beards tend also not to smell so weird.

Weird it's true to have that trace,

Traced not from body but from your face.

Faced up to it he did despite,

Despite all the teasers with their might.

Might you have put up with so much cheek?

Cheeky scamps calling you freak?

Freaky he may have been for sure,

But much worse things you can endure.

Enduring grit, few with more I know.

Know fewer still with face BO.

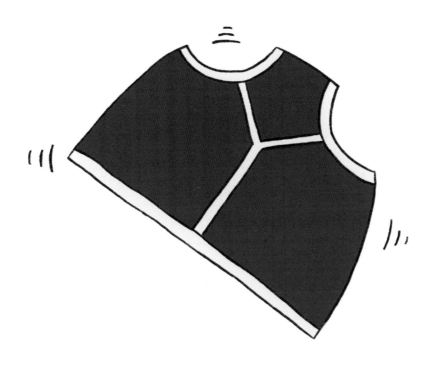

Somersaulting Underpants

Each night before I go to bed,

I flick my pants up to my head.

And as above my bonce they spin,

I nod them in the laundry bin.

I do this daily without fail,

I'll do it till I'm old and frail.

As there's little I can do with flair,

But somersault my underwear.

Sometimes with a floppy splat,

The pants become a kind of hat,

As they land right atop my noggin.

This ain't no easy sport I'm floggin'!

Go on then, why not have a try?

Start this evening, don't be shy.

But to play with clean-ish pants is wise,

So best avoided after exercise.

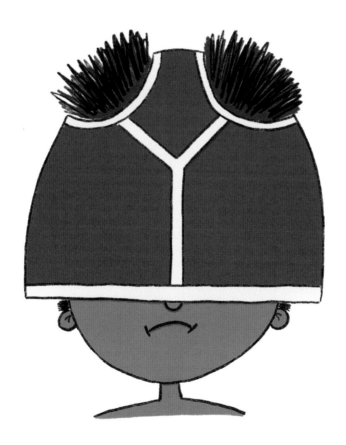

Playtime Twaddle

"Oh yeah?!" he said, "I'll wunket your head!

I'll frontle your daddy's Rolex!"

"Oh yeah?!" said I, "I'll gooble your eye!

If only you weren't wearing specs!"

← FRONTLING
    DEVICE

"Oh yeah?!" he spat, "I'll snoddy your hat!

And phling-phlong your pnippering boots!"

"Oh yeah?!" I spewed, "I'll klardle your food!

And jimp on both of your foots!"

"What's that?" said Eliza (play supervisor),

"You're making no sense, you pair."

"I'll yoodle his nose!" "I'll squittage his toes!"

"Oh yeah?!"

"Oh yeah?!"

"Oh yeah?!"

WATCH TOO
← NICE TO BE
HIDDEN BY
SLEEVE

PNIPPERING BOOT
BUY 1 GET 1 FREE

Bedtime Prayer

As I lay me down to sleep,

I pray the Lord my soul to keep.

And if he doesn't want my soul

He can have my sister's favourite doll.

About the author

Mikey O'Crikey grew up in a small town near London, England in the late-ish 20th century. He, his two brothers and sister all lived together with their mum and dad, who were a policeman and a dinner lady (not in that order).

They lived happily in their small house, which had a big garden where Mikey and his siblings loved to play; climbing the big silver birch, throwing grass darts at each other and peeing in the far corner bush when they couldn't be bothered to go inside to the toilet.

Outside of home, Mikey was a shy boy. But he was often happy with just his own thoughts for company. A daydreamer, he could be caught staring out the window as often as at the classroom board. He thinks this is where his fondness for coming up with silly rhymes and doodles had its foundation.

There will be more nonsense to come from Mikey O'Crikey. So keep your ear to the ground. Just not for long periods at a time; you wouldn't want to get a crick in your neck…

Find out more at **www.mikeyocrikey.com**

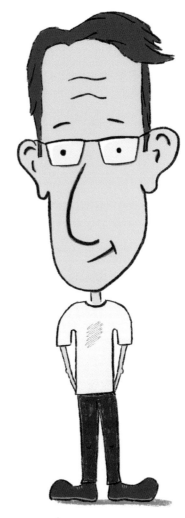

Self portrait

Self landscape

Before I go...

To those so very lovely few,

Who did an early book review,

I raise a glass, a mug, a cup,

And a really very big...

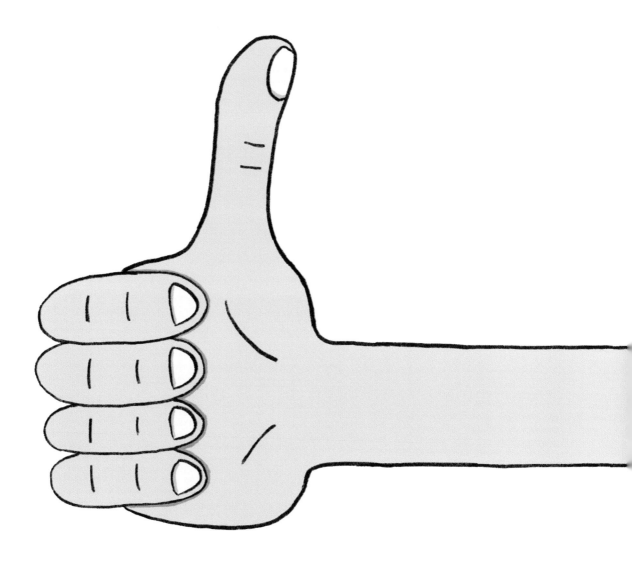

Extra special thanks to Clare for being an ever willing (figurative) guinea pig.

And to Wilma for being an ever willful (actual) kitten.

xxx

53

Printed in Great Britain
by Amazon